D0097878

Monte H Reger
Buffalo Okla.

The Tao of Cow

What Cows Teach Us

by Dolly Mu

Voyageur Press

Edited by Kari Cornell
Designed by Maria Friedrich
Printed in Hong Kong

01 02 03 04 05 5 4 3 2 1

Library of Congress Cataloging-in-
Publication Data

Mu, Dolly.
    The tao of cow : what cows teach us
    / Dolly Mu.
        p. cm.
    ISBN 0-89658-567-0 (alk. paper)
    1. Cows—Humor. 2. Cows—
    Quotations, maxims, etc. I. Title.

PN6231.C24 M82 2001
818'.602—dc21
                    2001026533

Distributed in Canada by Raincoast
Books, 9050 Shaughnessy Street,
Vancouver, B.C. V6P 6E5

Published by Voyageur Press, Inc.
123 North Second Street, P.O. Box 338, Stillwater, MN 55082 U.S.A.
651-430-2210, fax 651-430-2211
books@voyageurpress.com
www.voyageurpress.com

Educators, fundraisers, premium and gift buyers, publicists, and marketing managers: Looking for creative products and new sales ideas? Voyageur Press books are available at special discounts when purchased in quantities, and special editions can be created to your specifications. For details contact the marketing department at 800-888-9653.

On the endpapers: Engraving of cows from the December 1874 issue of the "American Agriculturist."

On the frontispiece: This proud cowboy steps right up to be photographed on his prized Watusi steer.

Page 2-3: New Salem Sue is one of the bigger Holsteins in New Salem, North Dakota. (Photograph © North Dakota Tourism Department)

Page 6-7: This big Hereford bull has the loving support of friends.

The Tao of Cow

What Cows Teach Us

Everyday is an opportunity to give of yourself.

Everyone lends a hand during the early morning milking. (Photograph © J.C. Allen & Son, Inc.)

Take time each day to bow down and pay homage to the glory of nature.

A Holstein cow settles down for an afternoon nap. (Photograph © Lynn M. Stone)

Stampede not through life, lest you miss the majesty of the world around you.

Western ranchers round up the herd for one last time.

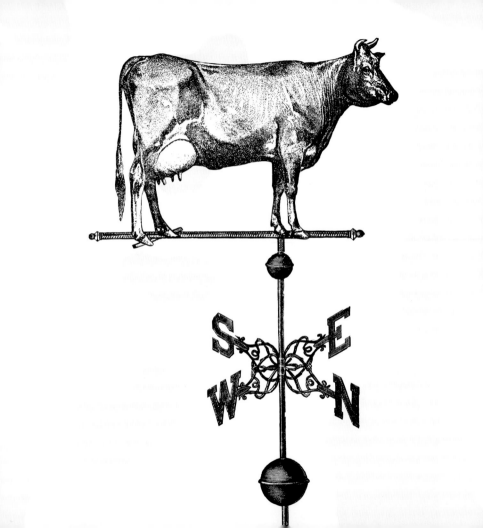

Always know which way the wind is blowing: Keep an open mind.

A shorthorned Jersey cow weather vane, as featured for sale in an 1883 catalog.

Judge not lest thou be judged.

Judges struggle to select the winning Guernsey cow from the 4-H club Guernsey Senior Calf Class. (Photograph © J.C. Allen & Son, Inc.)

Beware of false gods:
Things are not always as they seem.

J. Seivers Jr. patented this hunting decoy in the shape of a cow.
Notice how the head drops to make it look as if the cow is grazing.

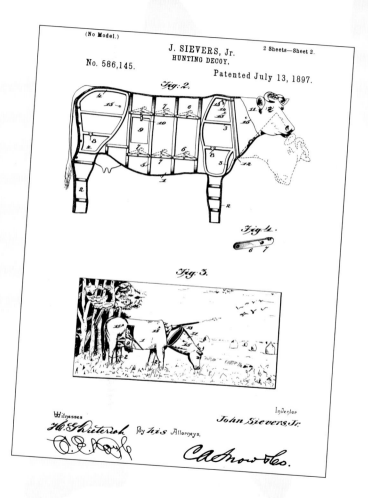

(No Model.)

2 Sheets—Sheet 2.

J. SIEVERS, Jr.
HUNTING DECOY.

No. 586,145.

Patented July 13, 1897.

Fig. 2.

Fig. 4.

Fig. 3.

Witnesses

H. Dieterich

By his Attorneys,

Inventor

John Sievers, Jr.

There are
greener pastures.

New Salem Sue, perched high above a North Dakota golf course, seems to be on the lookout for bad weather. (Photograph © North Dakota Tourism Department)

Sometimes the grass is exactly the same color green on the other side of the fence.

A group of Brown Swiss cows gather at a fence line.
(Photograph © J.C. Allen & Son, Inc.)

A steady mind and a steady hand will always hit the target.

Nice catch! This agile cat stands up on two paws to catch the milk from a cow's udder. (Photograph © Glenbow Archives, Calgary, Canada, NA-2084-75)

**Be stout of heart:
Life is not always as
bad as it appears.**

An old farmer shows off his
young bull.

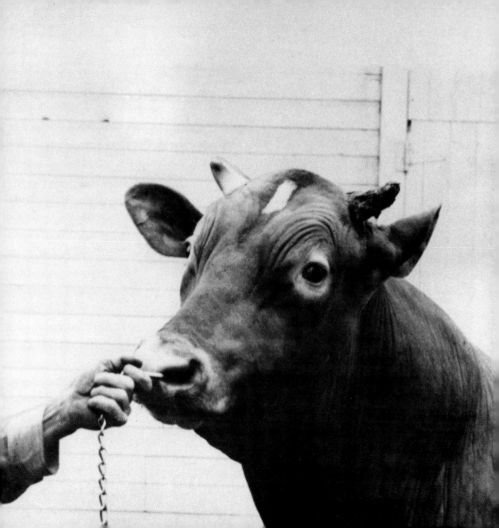

The balanced mind observes the world with both innocent acceptance and cautious doubt.

Now it's safe to say that you've had a really good look at a Guernsey cow.

(Photograph © Lynn M. Stone)

Believe not everything you hear.

These two Holstein cows appear to be shooting the breeze in a Vermont pasture. (Photograph © Lynn M. Stone)

Do not blow things out of proportion.

The December 1874 issue of the American Agriculturist featured this engraving of Shorthorn cattle.

Sometimes life's lessons are learned the hard way.

The full-color illustration of this none-too-happy cow first appeared in a 1956 International Harvester calendar.

Generosity cultivated in youth will blossom with age.

In this pastoral scene from the 1950s, a young girl feeds a calf fresh clover.

Cultivating curiosity keeps one young.

Calves investigate a barnyard newcomer. (Photograph © J.C. Allen & Son, Inc.)

With age comes wrinkles but also wisdom.

Brahman cattle, a breed from India, are known for their superior intellect.
(Photograph © J.C. Allen & Son, Inc.)

True beauty is more than just hide-deep.

This Ayrshire cow is beautiful through and through, wouldn't you agree? (Photograph © Lynn M. Stone)

Beauty is in the eye of the beholder.

Edwin Megargee crafted this exquisite portrait of a cow in 1925.

Always dress for success.

Dutch Belted cattle, originally bred by Dutch noblemen, wear a white
sash around their middle to distinguish them from more "common" breeds.
(Photograph © Keith Baum)

A beautiful smile will win you the world.

With its mop top do and sturdy build, the Scottish highland cow is one of the hardiest breeds in the world. (Photograph © Lynn M. Stone)

Beauty is enhanced by simple adornment.

Cows, dressed in their Sunday best, parade down a country road.
(Photograph © Lynn M. Stone)

But less is more.

A well-tagged Hereford calf. (Photograph © 2001 Bruce Fritz/ Fritz Photography)

Art is where you find it.

The watchful eyes of a modern Mona Lisa keep track of this Holstein herd in Cornell, Wisconsin. (Photograph © 2001 Bruce Fritz/Fritz Photography)

There is art inherent in even the most mundane endeavor.

A cow peers out from behind a hay stack shaped like a big mushroom.
(Photograph © Fred Hultstrand History in Pictures Collections,
NDSU, Fargo, ND)

Pulling your own weight is a virtue, but pulling the weight of others is saintly.

One saintly British white cow pulls a cartload of well-dressed children. (Photograph © Fred Hultstrand History in Pictures Collections, NDSU, Fargo, ND)

Cow karma dictates that a favor given will make you the favored one.

Mmmm . . . that's the spot. Two Ayrshire cows exchange favors. (Photograph © Lynn M. Stone)

The search for enlightenment will lead you to strange and mysterious places.

What this cow has discovered behind the tree is anyone's guess.
(Photograph © David Lorenz Winston)

Seek the sacred.

These cows lounge on Britain's Salisbury Plain, seemly bored by the popular tourist attraction of Stonehenge. (Photograph © David Lorenz Winston)

The longest road often leads to the greatest reward.

Holsteins take a stroll through a northern Wisconsin pasture.
(Photograph © J.C. Allen & Son, Inc.)

Often the simplest goal requires the greatest effort.

A Brown Swiss struggles to scratch an itch. (Photograph © Lynn M. Stone)

The pioneering spirit will lead you on untold adventures.

Two bulls await an itinerary. (Photograph © J.C. Allen & Son, Inc.)

If you run from your own shadow, you'll be running all of your days.

A Milking Shorthorn makes a mad dash down a Wisconsin hillside.
(Photograph © Lynn M. Stone)

The world needs both leaders and followers.

Three Brown Swiss cows cross a bridge over a mountain stream in Switzerland. (Photograph © Lynn M. Stone)

Blessings come in threes.

Milk from these three Brown Swiss cows is a blessing indeed.
(Photograph © 2001 Bruce Fritz/Fritz Photography)

Boasting isn't hollow if backed with accomplishment.

In this illustration from a 1954 Massey–Harris calendar, a 4-H prizewinner smiles for the camera.

The quality of your accomplishments determines the quality of your admirers.

Vice President Hubert Humphrey visits the children's barnyard at the Minnesota State Fair in 1965. (Photograph © Minnesota Historical Society)

Be swayed not by the will of others.

In this engraving from a 1878 issue of *Frank Leslie's Illustrated Newspaper*, cowboys drive a herd of Texas longhorn through Dodge City, Kansas.

Stand out from the herd . . . to thine own self always be true.

A majestic Brown Swiss stands alone. (Illustration courtesy of the Brown Swiss Cattle Breeders' Association)

Never be afraid to take the bull by the horns.

A rancher handles this big bull with caution. (Photograph © J.C. Allen & Son, Inc.)

Meet your destiny head on.

An up-close-and-personal look at a Brown Swiss.
(Photograph © Lynn M. Stone)

Butting heads won't necessarily make you see eye to eye.

A Milking Shorthorn goes head-to-head with a Holstein.
(Photograph © Lynn M. Stone)

Fight to maintain your dignity.

Before rodeos provided a venue for such activities, cowboys took turns riding bucking steers during roundups. (From an 1888 issue of "Frank Leslie's Illustrated Newspaper")

Be not afraid to explore other pastures.

This Holstein seems a little out of its element on the city streets. (Photograph © Glenbow Archives, Calgary, Canada, NA-2864-13233)

Sometimes you need to leave home to find yourself.

An Ayrshire cow braves the cold of an old-fashioned Midwestern winter.
(Photograph © Lynn M. Stone)

Sometimes you need to come home to find yourself.

And what an idyllic place to come home to! This illustration first appeared in a 1952 International Harvester calendar.

Foster Mothers of the Human Race

© HOARD'S DAIRYMAN

Motherhood is next to godliness.

The Brown Swiss, Ayrshire, Holstein, Guernsey, and Jersey cows pictured here represent the five breeds of dairy cattle.

Sometimes the old way is the best way.

It's always good to have the herd on hand when the new machinery fails. (Photograph © Glenbow Archives, Calgary, Canada, NA-101-35)

Special moments are fleeting but memories last forever.

Mom captures the proud mugs of her husband and son on film.

Sweet milk would sour at the honey of your smile

In a dark world,
a kind word
is a ray of light.

Quaint humor from a vintage
postcard.

Blessed are those who can laugh at themselves, for they will always be amused.

A Florida Cracker cow cracks a smile. (Photograph © Lynn M. Stone)

Lending your name to a cause close to your heart adds esteem to your name.

This vintage metal sign advertises H. P. Hood & Sons Milk.

Love freely given
is love gained.

A farmer gets a big smooch
from a good friend. (Photograph
© Minnesota State Fair
Collection)

Love is a many splendored thing.

A pair of friendly Guernsey cows nuzzle each other. (Photograph © Lynn M. Stone)

Be open to the kindness of others.

Brother and sister take turns brushing a Holstein calf. (Photograph © J.C. Allen & Son, Inc.)

Gracefully accepting admiration is the path to humility.

Visitors to New Salem, North Dakota, gaze up admiringly at New Salem Sue, the town's prized Holstein. (Photograph © North Dakota Tourism Department)

Taste life.

This Milking Shorthorn, one of a rare breed, has a wild tongue! (Photograph © Lynn M. Stone)

Be wary of biting off more than you can chew.

This Scottish Highland cow knows where to find a good snack.
(Photograph © David Lorenz Winston)

Feed tastes better with friends and fine fellowship makes a meal a feast.

A herd of Montana cows lines up at the trough. (Photograph © 2001 Bruce Fritz/Fritz Photography)

Vary your friends and vary your outlook.

A young farmer cuddles up with her favorite friends. (Photograph © J.C. Allen & Son, Inc.)

The words of a true friend
have the greatest meaning.

A couple of Guernsey cows chat over a repast of dandelions and grass.
(Photograph © Lynn M. Stone)

Peace with yourself leads to peace with others which leads to peace in the world.

Ayrshires spend a lazy afternoon grazing and resting. (Photograph © David Lorenz Winston)

AYRSHIRE COW.

Chapter XII.

THE GOOD MILKER.

Of all scrub stock the scrub milker is the worst.—Dorothy Tucker.

It is an accomplishment to be a rapid, thorough milker. It comes from early training, long practice and close intimacy with cows. Not only is precious time saved by a quick performance of the operation, but the cow's full capacity of production is encouraged. The precious liquid is drawn to the last drop, and the last drop is the richest of all.

The knack of milking is hard to describe; it comes by practice. The full teat is compressed by the hand in such a manner that the flow is downward, not back into the udder. A good milker will cause a perfect white shower to descend to the pail. In five minutes the udder is empty and the pail filled with froth-covered milk.

Good milking involves absolute cleanliness; a great many rapid milkers are unclean in their practices, that is, the milker intentionally moistens his hands with milk, and then proceeds to fill the pail.

The practice does not really make milking e_ _ ba and it is too much like using the pail as a wa_ _ ba It is altogether inexcusable.

A good cow is hard to find . . .

. . . But we may have found one in this fine Ayrshire cow.

Keep your feet on the ground but keep reaching for the sky.

A young member of the 4-H club dreams big in this illustration from a 1953 Massy-Harris calendar.

Do not waste time watching time.

A group of curious Holstein cows on a farm near Madison, Wisconsin wonder what's sitting on the fence post. And why is it ticking? (Photograph © 2001 Bruce Fritz/Fritz Photography)

The heart's song needs no audience.

A Vermont Ayrshire cow appears to have something to say (or sing).
(Photograph © Lynn M. Stone)

Set your sights high and you can reach the moon.

In the famous children's rhyme "Hey Diddle Diddle," the cow jumps over the moon.